I long to witness rapid growth and maturity of Christians in their faith. I firmly believe that an all-day church service has the potential to help accelerate this process and bring about profound transformation in the lives of believers.

- Mikee Shattuck

The modern Christian service, also known as the worship service or the Sunday service, has evolved over centuries, influenced by various historical, cultural, and theological factors. To understand its development, we need to explore the origins of Christian worship and trace its progression through key historical periods. The development of the Christian church service has undergone significant changes over the course of history. Here is a broad timeline highlighting some key milestones and shifts in Christian worship practices:

1st - 3rd centuries:

Early Christian worship primarily took place in homes, characterized by informal gatherings, communal prayers, Scripture reading, and the celebration of the Lord's Supper.

4th - 5th centuries:

Christianity became the official religion of the Roman Empire, leading to the construction of dedicated church buildings.
The liturgy became more structured and formalized, with the emergence of specific liturgical texts and rituals.
Sacraments, especially baptism and the Eucharist, gained increased importance within worship services.

6th - 10th centuries:

The liturgical traditions of the Eastern Orthodox Church and the Western Roman Catholic Church began to diverge.

The Eastern Orthodox Church developed a highly elaborate and symbolic liturgy, characterized by icons, incense, and intricate rituals.

The Western Roman Catholic Church focused on the Roman Rite, which included Gregorian chant, a more simplified liturgy, and an emphasis on the Eucharist.

11th - 16th centuries:

The Medieval period saw the rise of monastic orders, leading to the development of monastic liturgical practices.

The Latin Mass became the dominant form of worship in the Western Roman Catholic Church, with prayers and Scripture readings conducted in Latin.

The Protestant Reformation in the 16th century brought changes to Christian worship, with reformers advocating for the use of vernacular languages, congregational participation, and a greater emphasis on preaching.

17th - 18th centuries:

The emergence of Protestant denominations led to further diversification in worship practices.

Hymnody gained popularity, and the use of hymns in congregational singing became widespread. The Puritan movement emphasized simplicity in worship, focusing on preaching, prayer, and the reading of Scripture.

19th - 20th centuries:

The rise of revivalist movements, such as the Great Awakening, brought about changes in worship style, with an increased emphasis on emotional experiences, altar calls, and evangelistic preaching.

The liturgical renewal movement in the 20th century sought to incorporate elements of ancient liturgy into contemporary worship practices, influencing both Protestant and Catholic traditions. The Charismatic movement introduced more expressive forms of worship, including contemporary music, speaking in tongues, and a focus on spiritual gifts.
21st century:

Worship practices have become more diverse and eclectic, reflecting the cultural contexts and preferences of different Christian communities....

Introduction: Reimagining Sunday Service

Since the earliest days of Christianity, believers have gathered together for worship, fellowship, teaching, and prayer. In modern times, these gatherings have typically taken the form of a weekly Sunday service - a structured, timed event where congregants come together to worship God, listen to biblical teachings, and engage with their community.

The traditional Sunday service has a rhythm, a flow that has served us well for generations. It provides a space for worship through hymns and contemporary Christian music, it creates a platform for pastors and leaders to share the Word of God, and it fosters a sense of community among attendees.

However, with the ever-evolving societal and generational norms, there's been an increasing need for a space that not only accommodates these shifts but also empowers individuals to connect with God and their community on their terms. A space that breaks down the time constraints of traditional services and allows for a deeper exploration of faith, fellowship, and personal spiritual growth.

This book introduces a revolutionary concept - an all-day Sunday service. Imagine a space where the doors of the church are open all day, inviting you to participate in worship, learn from diverse voices, engage in deep fellowship, and partake in personal prayer, all at your own pace. A space where you can come and go as you wish, for as little or as long as you like, and truly immerse yourself in whatever spiritual activities resonate with you the most.

As we delve into this concept, we will explore its three main components - the Worship Room, the Teaching Room, and the Fellowship Room, each providing unique opportunities to engage with your faith. We will guide you through the implementation process, anticipate the benefits, and present potential challenges along with their solutions.

The goal is to cultivate a richer, more engaging, and more personal experience of Sunday service - an experience that reflects the diverse needs of our current generation, and ultimately, brings us closer to God and each other. Welcome to a new era of church service.

Chapter 1: The Traditional Sunday Service

The typical Sunday service follows a structured format, which although varies slightly across denominations, usually contains several consistent elements:

Opening Worship: Services often begin with a time of worship, a tradition dating back to biblical times (Psalms 100:2). Through hymns, rooted in centuries-old tradition, or contemporary Christian music, inspired by modern culture and contexts, the congregation is invited to join in corporate worship. This worship session is led by a choir, a band, or an individual musician, making the church resound with harmonious voices raised in praise. According to the Psalms, "Enter his gates with thanksgiving and his courts with praise; give thanks to him and praise his name" (Psalms 100:4). Opening worship is designed to set a spiritual tone for the service and prepare the hearts of the attendees to receive the Word of God.

Biblical Teaching or Sermon: At the heart of most services is the sermon or biblical teaching. This is when a pastor, minister, or church leader delivers a message inspired by scripture passages. The tradition of preaching dates back to Jesus himself, who was known to teach in synagogues and public places (Luke 4:43-44). Preaching is a central duty of church leaders as per Paul's exhortation to Timothy to "Preach the word; be prepared in season and out of season; correct, rebuke and encourage—with great patience and careful instruction" (2 Timothy 4:2). These teachings typically offer an interpretation or application of the scriptures relevant to contemporary life, serving as a spiritual guide for believers.

Prayers: Prayers are an integral part of any service, reflecting the biblical admonition to "pray without ceasing" (1 Thessalonians 5:17). These prayers often encompass a broad range of topics, including confession (1 John 1:9), thanksgiving (Philippians 4:6), and intercession for the church community and the wider world (1 Timothy 2:1-2). By praying together, the congregation can express a collective faith and share their joys, hopes, and concerns.

Communion or Eucharist: Depending on the denomination, some churches include communion or the Eucharist as part of the service, commemorating the Last Supper of Jesus (Luke 22:19-20). This sacrament symbolizes Christ's sacrifice, reminding believers of His love and encouraging them to live a life reflecting His teachings.

Fellowship: Services usually conclude with a time of fellowship. This practice aligns with the early Christian community's practice as described in Acts 2:42, "They devoted themselves to the apostles' teaching and to fellowship, to the breaking of bread and to prayer." This fellowship period often casual and unstructured, allows attendees to socialize, share experiences, discuss the sermon, or simply enjoy each other's company. This time builds a stronger sense of community among believers, allowing them to "encourage one another and build each other up" (1 Thessalonians 5:11).

In each of these elements, the traditional Sunday service offers valuable opportunities for worship, learning, and community building. However, as we will explore in subsequent chapters, a different approach may offer a more personalized, flexible, and potentially enriching spiritual experience.

This model of Sunday service is familiar and comfortable for many. It provides a balance of worship, teaching, and community engagement. The structure gives attendees a predictable flow of events and a solid foundation for their Sunday spiritual experience.

While the traditional Sunday service has been a mainstay in Christian worship, it is not without its limitations. A key constraint is the rigidity of timing. Traditionally, services are held at a specific time, often in the morning or early afternoon. This time-bound model can exclude individuals who are unable to commit to this schedule due to work commitments, family obligations, or even differences in personal rhythms and routines. As our society shifts towards a 24/7 model, with people working and living on a variety of schedules, the once universally convenient Sunday morning time slot may no longer serve everyone equally.

Moreover, the structured format of the traditional service may not cater to the individual spiritual needs of all attendees. The model provides a 'one-size-fits-all' approach that may not resonate with everyone, particularly those who seek a deeper or different kind of engagement. For instance, some may prefer extended periods of worship through music, while others may yearn for more time dedicated to quiet reflection or in-depth bible study. The traditional format offers little flexibility for attendees to engage in the aspects of the service that they find most spiritually fulfilling.

Furthermore, the delivery of the sermon, which is typically one-way, may limit interaction and engagement from attendees. While this mode of delivery allows for a clear, uninterrupted message from the pastor or church leader, it often turns the congregation into passive recipients rather than active participants. The lack of opportunity for dialogue or exchange of ideas can limit the attendees' understanding or connection to the teachings, making it difficult for some to relate the teachings to their own experiences.

These challenges are increasingly significant given the societal and generational shifts towards greater personalization, flexibility, and active participation. Today's congregants, particularly younger generations, desire worship experiences that accommodate their personal needs, preferences, and schedules. They seek spaces that allow them to be active participants in their faith journey, rather than passive observers.

In response to these emerging needs, we propose a new concept: the all-day Sunday service. This innovative approach to Sunday worship offers a dynamic, inclusive, and individually tailored experience. It allows attendees to engage with their faith at their own pace, in their own preferred manner, and at a time that suits their schedule.

In the all-day Sunday service, the church doors remain open all day. The structure is flexible, allowing individuals to delve deeper into worship, teaching, prayer, or fellowship according to their own needs and desires. This approach provides a solution to the limitations of traditional Sunday service and offers a fresh, modern take on communal worship, fitting for the changing dynamics of our society. In the subsequent chapters, we will delve into the specifics of how this all-day Sunday service can be implemented and the many benefits it can bring to the Christian community.

The all-day Sunday service heralds a transformative approach to communal worship. In this model, the church doors are not just opened for a few hours but remain welcoming throughout the entire day. This extended accessibility offers a solution to the scheduling conflicts faced by many congregants under the traditional structure.

In this model of or "service", the traditional components of the service are deconstructed and expanded upon. Individuals are granted the flexibility to delve deeper into aspects of their faith that resonate most with them, be it worship, teaching, prayer, or fellowship. The service structure is not rigid but fluid, allowing attendees to move organically between different activities according to their needs, preferences, and the promptings of the Holy Spirit.

Imagine a worship room where music—both hymns and contemporary Christian songs—fills the air all day long, inviting anyone who wishes to join in praising God through song. Picture a teaching room where a variety of speakers, representing all walks of life, share their testimonies and teachings from the Bible, igniting meaningful discussions. Visualize a serene space dedicated to prayer, where anyone can offer or receive prayers at any time. Lastly, envision a fellowship area that facilitates relaxed and genuine interactions, fostering deeper connections among believers.

This approach, while it retains the core components of traditional Sunday service, offers a fresh, modern take on communal worship. It adapts to the changing dynamics of our society by offering greater personalization, flexibility, and active participation. The all-day Sunday service emphasizes that the church isn't just a place we visit, but a vibrant community we actively participate in and shape according to our collective and individual spiritual journeys.

In subsequent chapters, we will delve deeper into the specifics of the all-day Sunday service. We will discuss the practicalities of implementing such a model, explore its benefits, and highlight real-world examples of its application. We will explore how this concept can transform not only Sunday services but also the wider Christian community, bringing forth a new era of inclusive, flexible, and participatory worship.

Chapter 2: The Need for Change

Over time, society evolves. Our ways of thinking, our daily routines, and even our ways of interacting with one another continually shift. These changes are brought about by various factors, including technological advancements, changing cultural norms, and evolving generational attitudes and expectations. For the church to continue being a relevant and vital institution in people's lives, it must acknowledge and respond to these changes. This chapter will delve into the societal, cultural, and generational shifts that necessitate a reconsideration of the traditional Sunday service model and explore why a more flexible, open, and interactive service may be the answer.

Societal Shifts

In today's modern world, the patterns of people's lives have significantly diverged from the traditional norms that once governed society. The classic nine-to-five workday, once a cornerstone of professional life, is being increasingly supplanted by a more varied spectrum of work patterns.

The rise of flexible work schedules has been a game-changer. Now, employees can often customize their work hours to better align with their personal lives and productivity peaks. This flexibility, while a tremendous advantage, also means that many people may be working or otherwise occupied during the traditional Sunday morning service hours.

The evolution of work doesn't stop there. The gig economy, characterized by freelancing and short-term contracts, has exploded in recent years. The convenience of working on-demand and the lure of being one's own boss has led many people to embrace this type of work. However, the gig economy operates 24/7, making conventional work hours obsolete for many.

In addition, a surge in night shifts, remote work, and international collaboration in an increasingly globalized economy means that people are often working unconventional hours. For those working late into the night or starting their workdays before dawn to collaborate with colleagues in different time zones, attending a Sunday morning service may not be feasible.

Moreover, societal change isn't just about work. The structure of our personal lives has also changed. Single-parent households, adults pursuing education alongside work, and an increase in multigenerational homes have led to complex personal schedules that might conflict with traditional service times.

The traditional Sunday morning service, although cherished, may inadvertently exclude those entangled in these contemporary societal shifts. To ensure that everyone has the opportunity to participate in church services, a new model must be considered: the all-day Sunday service.

By keeping the church doors open all day, we accommodate these changing patterns and rhythms. Whether someone works the night shift and sleeps till noon or is a freelancer juggling multiple gigs, the all-day service ensures that everyone can find a time to participate in communal worship. The church becomes an accessible spiritual haven for all, irrespective of their work schedule or personal circumstances. It truly embodies the inclusivity at the heart of the Christian faith.

Cultural Shifts

In the culture of the 21st century, customization is king. With the proliferation of digital technology and the ease of global communication, there has been a significant cultural shift towards more personalized experiences across various sectors of life.

This shift is readily apparent in the consumer realm. Online shopping platforms offer personalized recommendations based on buying history and browsing behavior. Music streaming services create custom playlists that cater to individual tastes. Even our social media feeds are curated according to our interests, activities, and connections.

A similar trend can be observed in the world of entertainment. On-demand streaming platforms allow viewers to choose what to watch and when, rather than being tied to television networks' schedules. Video games offer personalized experiences where players can shape their virtual world.

The realm of education hasn't been immune to this cultural shift either. Modern pedagogical methods highlight personalized learning plans that cater to each student's learning style, pace, and interests. Online courses and platforms allow learners to pick and choose topics they're interested in, study at their own pace, and even select their preferred method of learning, be it through video lectures, reading materials, or interactive quizzes.

This emphasis on personalization mirrors a broader cultural desire for experiences that resonate with individual preferences, needs, and circumstances. People today value their ability to shape their experiences and steer their journeys, rather than fitting into a one-size-fits-all mold.

It's only logical that this desire for personalization extends to spiritual life. Many seek a faith experience that speaks to their personal journey, that respects their individual rhythms, and allows them to connect with God in ways that are most meaningful and authentic to them.

A more flexible and open Sunday service aligns perfectly with this cultural trend. By offering an array of worship experiences - from praise music to testimonies, teaching, prayer, and fellowship - an all-day service allows individuals to tailor their worship experience to their needs and preferences. It allows for deep, personal engagement with faith, rather than a passive, one-size-fits-all approach.

In essence, the all-day Sunday service offers a way to keep faith relevant in a culture that values personalization and individual journeys. It ensures that the church remains a vibrant, dynamic space where each person can seek, experience, and express their faith in a way that is profoundly personal and deeply meaningful.

Generational Shifts

The faith journey is deeply personal and varies from person to person. Even more so, it can vary significantly between generations. Different generations bring different expectations, attitudes, and desires to their faith practices. Understanding these generational differences is critical to ensuring that the church remains relevant and engaging for all its members.

Research suggests that younger generations - particularly millennials and Generation Z - approach their faith with a distinct set of values. One of these is a strong emphasis on authenticity. In a world often criticized for being superficial and image-driven, these younger generations crave genuineness in their spiritual experiences. They seek a faith that is lived out and made real in daily life, not just professed in words.

Furthermore, millennials and Gen Z members value community. However, their concept of community goes beyond mere social interactions; it encompasses a shared sense of purpose, mutual support, and collective engagement in meaningful activities. They are drawn to communities that allow them to make a difference, that involve them in the collective mission, and that facilitate deep, meaningful connections with others.

Active participation is another significant value for these generations. They want to be part of the conversation, to contribute their thoughts and ideas, and to play an active role in their faith practices. They are less likely to be satisfied with a passive experience of receiving a one-way sermon. Instead, they yearn for interactive, participatory forms of worship that allow them to engage their faith actively.

An all-day Sunday service is ideally suited to cater to these desires and expectations. By offering various activities throughout the day, this model of worship allows for a more interactive and engaging experience. Those attending can choose from a variety of ways to participate, from music-led worship to communal prayer, learning through testimonies and teachings, and engaging in fellowship.

Moreover, an all-day service facilitates authenticity by offering a space where faith is continuously lived out through various activities. It nurtures community by offering shared experiences and spaces for meaningful interactions. It fosters active participation by encouraging attendees to take part in prayer, learning, and fellowship according to their own timing, needs, and preferences.

In this way, the all-day Sunday service can engage younger generations in a manner that aligns with their values and expectations, offering them a fulfilling and enriching worship experience that resonates with their desire for authenticity, community, and active participation.

The shift from a traditional Sunday service to a more flexible, open, and interactive all-day service brings a host of benefits for both individuals and the church community as a whole. These benefits span various aspects of the spiritual journey, meeting attendees where they are and empowering them to engage with their faith in deeply personal and meaningful ways.

Firstly, flexibility is a significant advantage of an all-day service. In a society characterized by varying work schedules and diverse personal commitments, having the option to attend a service at any time throughout the day is a major boon. This flexibility respects the differing rhythms of people's lives, ensuring that everyone can partake in the church service regardless of their schedule. Not being bound by a set service time removes a potential barrier to participation, making the church experience accessible to all.

In addition to timing, the all-day service offers flexibility in terms of engagement. Attendees can choose which aspects of the service to participate in based on their spiritual needs and desires at that time. Whether one feels called to lift their voice in song, immerse themselves in biblical teaching, offer or receive prayers, or simply fellowship with others, the choice is theirs. This model respects and caters to the diversity of spiritual needs within the congregation, allowing each individual to tailor their worship experience in a way that resonates most with them.

An open and inclusive environment is another major benefit of this model. By offering various activities throughout the day and allowing attendees to come and go as they please, the church cultivates an atmosphere of openness and inclusivity. Everyone is welcome, everyone is included, and everyone can find a space and activity that speaks to them.

An all-day service also encourages interaction and active participation, fostering a sense of community and belonging. When attendees have the opportunity to pray for others, to share their testimonies, to discuss biblical teachings, or simply to connect with fellow believers, they become active contributors to the community. This active engagement can deepen one's sense of connection and ownership towards their faith and their church community.

A flexible, open, and interactive all-day service offers a dynamic, inclusive, and participatory worship experience. It respects the diversity of spiritual needs and rhythms of life within the congregation, fosters a vibrant and engaged community, and empowers individuals to experience their faith in deeply personal and meaningful ways. The result is a church experience that is as diverse, dynamic, and individual as the members it serves.

In the next chapter, we will discuss how an all-day Sunday service can be implemented, exploring the various components of such a service and how they can work together to create an enriching and inclusive worship experience.

Chapter 3: An All-Day Sunday Service - An Introduction:

Picture this: The sun breaks the horizon and ushers in the dawn of a new Sunday. As light begins to pour into the city streets, the doors of a local church swing open, inviting the early risers in. This is not just another Sunday service; it is the beginning of an all-day spiritual retreat, an experience that invites attendees to connect on their own terms.

This is an all-day Sunday service, an innovative concept that reimagines the traditional church experience.

For many, the traditional church service, while deeply cherished, follows a rhythm and structure that may not resonate with everyone's spiritual needs. While its predictability provides comfort, it may also unintentionally limit the avenues through which individuals can explore their faith. This is where the vision of an all-day Sunday service steps in, offering a fresh perspective that aligns with the evolving spiritual landscape of the modern world.

This all-day Sunday service doesn't simply stretch the standard one or two-hour service into a day-long event. It is not an exercise in endurance, but in flexibility, diversity, and autonomy. The idea expands the horizons of what a church service can be, offering a variety of ways to engage with God and the community, and allowing attendees to chart their own spiritual journey within the broader context of communal worship.

Imagine a church where you can join a group engaged in enthusiastic worship at any time of the day, their songs of praise forming a melodic backdrop to the day's activities. Here, worship is not confined to the first half hour of a service; it becomes a continual offering of love and devotion, a dynamic soundtrack that underscores the entire day.

Picture a space in this church dedicated to quiet reflection and prayer, away from the buzz of the world. Envision 'Prayer Chairs' where anyone can sit at any time to receive prayer or offer it. These chairs, available throughout the day, invite an ongoing dialogue with God, moving prayer from being a specific segment in a service to an accessible conversation that can be joined at any time.

Then, imagine a room where teachings and testimonies aren't limited to a single sermon but are presented throughout the day by different voices, each bringing their unique experiences and perspectives. In this space, wisdom is shared and lessons are learned in a setting that encourages interaction and dialogue. With new speakers rotating attendees can immerse themselves in a variety of teachings and testimonies, choosing which ones they wish to attend.

And finally, envision a place of fellowship, where attendees can relax, maybe share a meal, engage in rich conversations, or simply enjoy each other's company. This room becomes a living room for the church community, a place where relationships are nurtured, stories are shared, and a sense of belonging is fostered.

The all-day Sunday service breaks down the walls of convention, blurring the lines between worship, teaching, prayer, and fellowship. It encourages active participation over passive observation and cultivates a sense of autonomy and personal responsibility in one's spiritual journey. It offers an inclusive environment that respects and celebrates diversity, recognizing that every person's path to God is unique.

Above all, the all-day Sunday service is a testament to the transforming power of faith. It represents a church that is willing to evolve, to look beyond tradition and create a space that meets the needs of a diverse and changing congregation. It is a bold step towards a more engaging, more personal, and more empowering approach to communal worship, a step that could, quite possibly, redefine the way we do church in the modern world.

In the all-day Sunday service, every hour holds a possibility, every room a spiritual adventure. The experience unfolds at a pace set by the individual, offering numerous opportunities to connect with God and the community throughout the day. This is a vision that extends the concept of church beyond a service, transforming it into a vibrant spiritual hub that remains open and active all day. It's an ambitious idea, a challenging undertaking, and, for many, a long-awaited answer to a call for change. **Welcome to the all-day Sunday service, where faith isn't scheduled, but lived.**

Chapter 4: The Worship Room

The Worship Room stands at the heart of the all-day Sunday service, a room dedicated to unending praise, worship, and prayer. Regardless of a church's size or resources, the Worship Room can be crafted to reflect the spirit of continuous devotion and heartfelt intercession.

For smaller churches, it may not be feasible to have a live band or choir present throughout the day. However, worship is not confined to live music. Recorded worship music, carefully selected to foster an atmosphere of praise and devotion, can be played throughout the day. For those who prefer a quieter environment for prayer and worship, a portion of the day can be dedicated to silent prayer, meditation, or soft instrumental music.

Prayer chairs offer a physical and symbolic space for open-ended intercession. In smaller churches, a few chairs set aside for this purpose could serve this function. Larger churches might designate a specific section of the room for this purpose, with several chairs or prayer benches. The key is that anyone can sit in these chairs anytime they wish, opening themselves up for someone to pray with them.

The prayer chair concept is reminiscent of Jesus's words in Matthew 18:20, "For where two or three gather in my name, there am I with them." This is the essence of the prayer chair - it's not about the chair itself, but the connection, the prayer, and the presence of God invoked through prayer. The concept encourages mutual support and spiritual interaction among the congregation, underscoring the biblical tenets of intercession and community.

In larger churches, a rotating team of dedicated prayer ministers can be on hand to pray with those in the prayer chairs. In smaller congregations, this role can be taken by any willing member of the church. The invitation is open to everyone, no matter their age or spiritual maturity, to step into the role of an intercessor, fostering a sense of shared spiritual responsibility and deepening the community's bonds.

The Worship Room, in its multifaceted nature, serves as a sanctuary for the spiritual seeker, a refuge for the weary, and a communal haven where praise and worship to the Most High are as ceaseless as the tide. This concept draws its inspiration from the apostle John's vision in the Book of Revelation, where the heavenly host ceaselessly proclaims the holiness of God: "And the four living creatures, each of them with six wings, are full of eyes all around and within, and day and night they never cease to say, 'Holy, holy, holy, is the Lord God Almighty, who was and is and is to come!'" (Revelation 4:8).

Within the Worship Room, we echo this eternal praise, creating a miniature mirror of the heavenly spectacle here on Earth. This isn't a room merely for ritual or obligation; rather, it's a pulsating hub of adoration, petition, and connection. The Worship Room invites us into an intimate dance with divinity, an opportunity to engage in the dynamic ebb and flow of giving and receiving blessings through praise, worship, and intercessory prayer.

The beauty of the Worship Room lies not just in its purpose, but also in its accessibility. Whether you find yourself drawn in for a fleeting moment in the midst of a bustling day or yearn for extended hours of meditative prayer and worship, the room adapts to your needs. It is not bound by the clock, for the divine dialogue it houses is timeless. It's a living testament to a faith that's not dictated by hours and minutes, but by the longing and intensity of spiritual connection.

The Worship Room shatters the conventional image of a rigid and regimented prayer service. Instead, it emphasizes a personal and flexible approach to worship. Here, you won't find yourself constrained by the expected etiquettes of traditional prayer services, but encouraged to express your devotion in a way that resonates with your spiritual rhythm. You can sing, kneel, stand, or simply sit in silent contemplation – the room does not demand uniformity in worship but celebrates the diversity of spiritual expressions.

The Worship Room is also a beacon of community and shared spiritual experiences. The shared prayers, the collective voices lifted in song, the silent yet profound sense of unity in purpose, all contribute to forging deeper bonds within the church community. It's a testament to the transformative power of collective worship, underpinned by the belief that when we come together in God's name, He is present among us.

Chapter 5: The Teaching Room

The Teaching Room, in its essence, is a vibrant, dynamic, and diverse space for the congregation to engage with the Word of God and hear the testimonies of fellow believers. Implementing a Teaching Room in an all-day Sunday service might vary in execution depending on the size of the church, but the core elements of variety, rotation, and real-life applications can be carried across any context.

In a smaller church, the Teaching Room may simply be a quiet corner or separate room where attendees can gather to hear a member of the congregation share their testimony or a reflection on a biblical passage. The notion here is to rotate speakers every 30 minutes, ensuring a fresh voice and perspective is always on offer. This doesn't necessarily require a large pool of speakers. A smaller community might have members speak multiple times throughout the day, each time offering a different reflection or sharing another facet of their faith journey.

Certainly, smaller churches will face unique challenges in implementing the all-day Teaching Room, particularly in having a continuous rotation of speakers. Yet, creative solutions can ensure that the spirit of diverse and ongoing teachings is maintained, such as through the use of recorded videos.

A way to overcome the potential shortage of live speakers is to curate a library of pre-recorded videos of sermons, reflections, and testimonies. These videos could be produced by members of the congregation or sourced from respected Christian speakers and teachers, online platforms, or even other church communities willing to share their resources.

These recorded videos could be played in between live speakers, ensuring that there is always something edifying on offer in the Teaching Room. They provide an excellent way to bring in a diverse range of voices, experiences, and teachings, even from across the globe. This diversity further enriches the spiritual experience and broadens the understanding of attendees.

Moreover, having these recordings gives the church the flexibility to tailor the content to the specific needs and interests of their congregation. For instance, during certain times of the day, the videos could be geared more towards children or youth, or focus on particular themes or parts of the Bible.

Another approach could be to invite members of the congregation to share their testimonies or teachings via pre-recorded videos. This might be particularly appealing for those who are nervous about speaking live, or for those who cannot be present on Sundays but still wish to contribute. These videos could be collected and screened throughout the day, interspersed with live speakers and other recorded content.

Furthermore, to create an interactive environment, following each video, there could be a facilitated discussion. A church leader or volunteer could help the group unpack the teachings, prompting attendees to share their reflections and questions, fostering a dynamic learning environment.

By leveraging technology and recorded content, even small churches can create a robust, engaging, and diverse Teaching Room experience. The result is a dynamic exchange of wisdom and experiences that speaks into the hearts and minds of all those present, fostering deeper understanding and more personal connection with the teachings of Jesus.

For larger churches, there may be the option of dedicating an entire room or even multiple rooms for this purpose. Here, the larger congregation provides the opportunity to feature a wider variety of speakers, including church leaders, regular members, and even guest speakers from the broader Christian community. The key element is not the size or the number of available speakers, but the intentionality in creating an environment that encourages diversity of expression and thought.

The concept of the Teaching Room is centered around learning from a variety of voices and experiences, acknowledging that God works uniquely in each of our lives. Therefore, creating a space for these stories to be told can enrich the faith journey of the listeners. Additionally, the opportunity for any willing church member to share their experiences or insights promotes a more egalitarian approach, reminiscent of the New Testament church, where each member played a part in building up the community (1 Corinthians 14:26).

The teaching content should reflect the diversity of the speakers, ranging from theological reflections, scriptural interpretations, and teachings on Christian living, to personal testimonies of God's work in their lives. The aim is to foster an environment of learning and sharing that allows individuals to glean wisdom from various perspectives, apply it to their lives, and see the multifaceted ways God operates in His people.

It's worth noting that implementing an all-day rotation of speakers will require planning and coordination. This may involve creating a schedule of speakers for the day, providing guidelines for the type of content that can be shared, and ensuring there's technical support if required. Encouraging church members to pre-register as speakers can also be beneficial, ensuring that there are enough speakers to fill the rotation and allowing for better planning.

For those unable to physically be present, the teachings can be livestreamed or recorded and shared later, allowing even more individuals to benefit from the shared wisdom. This can be an excellent way to involve homebound members of the congregation or those who may be unable to attend the Sunday service due to work or other commitments.

The Teaching Room provides a unique opportunity for individuals within the congregation who have been blessed with the gift of teaching to truly thrive. As outlined in Romans 12:6-8, Christians have different gifts, and those who can teach should embrace and use that gift. The Teaching Room, with its rotating schedule of speakers, creates a platform where these individuals can step forward and use their God-given talents.

This idea aligns with the biblical concept of the body of Christ, where every member has a unique role to play (1 Corinthians 12:27). In a traditional Sunday service, the teaching typically comes from one pastor or a small team of church leaders. In contrast, the all-day service model invites a wider range of individuals to contribute their insights and understanding, truly representing the diverse body of Christ.

Moreover, having a larger pool of teachers and speakers also ensures a wide range of topics, perspectives, and styles, making the Word more accessible to a broader audience. Someone who might not connect with one person's teaching style could be profoundly impacted by another's. Thus, the congregation as a whole can benefit from this wealth of diversity.

But it's not just the listeners who stand to gain. The individuals with the gift of teaching also experience personal spiritual growth through this process. Preparing a teaching or testimony encourages them to delve deeper into the Word, enhancing their understanding and relationship with God. Furthermore, by stepping up to share their insights and experiences, they are practicing obedience, humility, and service, which are key to spiritual maturity.

The Teaching Room also offers an environment where new or emerging teachers can develop their skills. They can learn from more experienced speakers and gradually gain confidence in a supportive, community-centered setting. Over time, this can lead to a strong team of competent, committed teachers who can contribute not only to the Sunday services but also to other church activities and ministries, enriching the overall spiritual life of the congregation.

Thus, the all-day Sunday service model, particularly the Teaching Room component, can be instrumental in fostering a vibrant, interactive, and spiritually nourishing environment. It acknowledges and celebrates the different gifts within the church, encourages active participation, and provides opportunities for individuals to grow in their faith and service.

Chapter 6: The Fellowship Room

The Fellowship Room is a space within the all-day Sunday service dedicated to fostering community, connection, and meaningful relationships. Regardless of the size of a church, the Fellowship Room can be adapted to cater to the needs and resources of the congregation.

For smaller churches, the Fellowship Room can be a designated area within the church building, transformed into a warm and inviting space where attendees can gather, chat, and enjoy each other's company. It could be a cozy corner with comfortable seating, coffee tables, and refreshments, providing an atmosphere conducive to relaxed conversations and fellowship. This space allows for the cultivation of deep relationships, where church members can share their joys, struggles, and experiences, providing mutual support and encouragement.

In larger churches, the Fellowship Room may require a more spacious setting to accommodate a larger number of attendees. This room can be designed to include various zones or sections, each catering to different activities or interests. For example, there could be a section for casual conversations, a space for group discussions or Bible studies, and even a designated area for games and recreational activities. These zones allow individuals to engage in fellowship according to their preferences, ensuring that everyone can find a place to connect and belong.

Furthermore, technology can play a significant role in facilitating fellowship in churches of all sizes. For instance, even smaller churches can consider creating online communities or social media groups to foster connections beyond the physical gathering. This provides an opportunity for individuals to engage in ongoing conversations, share prayer requests, and support one another throughout the week. It allows the bonds formed in the Fellowship Room to extend beyond the confines of a single day, strengthening the sense of community and unity.

To encourage deeper engagement and intentional fellowship, churches can organize structured activities or programs within the Fellowship Room. This could include small group discussions on specific topics, workshops on various aspects of Christian living, or even interactive sessions where attendees can share their testimonies and experiences. These activities can be facilitated by church leaders or volunteers who help guide the discussions and ensure everyone feels included and valued.

It's important to remember that the Fellowship Room is not solely about casual conversations or socializing, but also about providing a space for deeper spiritual connections. Churches can encourage the formation of mentorship or discipleship relationships within this room, where more experienced believers can invest in the lives of newer members or individuals seeking guidance. This intentional pairing can lead to significant spiritual growth and personal transformation.

Additionally, the Fellowship Room can be a place of outreach and evangelism. Churches can create welcoming environments where visitors or newcomers feel comfortable engaging with church members and learning more about the Christian faith. It provides an opportunity for individuals to ask questions, seek guidance, and explore their own spiritual journey within a supportive and non-judgmental setting.

Regardless of size, the Fellowship Room serves as a vital component of the all-day Sunday service, nurturing a sense of belonging, fostering deeper relationships, and creating opportunities for personal and spiritual growth. It is a space where laughter is shared, burdens are lifted, and lives are impacted. Churches of all sizes can adapt and customize the Fellowship Room to fit their unique contexts, ultimately creating an environment where the body of Christ can thrive in love and fellowship.

Chapter 7: Families & Children

When considering the implementation of an all-day Sunday service, it is important to address the needs of families and provide a supportive environment that allows them to fully engage in the experience. This includes considerations for child care and creating opportunities for families to stay together throughout the day.

In larger churches that have the facilities and resources, offering child care services can be a valuable addition to the all-day Sunday service. This ensures that parents can actively participate in worship, teaching, prayer, and fellowship, knowing that their children are well cared for in a safe and nurturing environment. Dedicated child care areas staffed by trained volunteers or professionals can provide age-appropriate activities, allowing children to learn and have fun while their parents participate in the service.

To further enhance the family experience, churches can incorporate family-friendly elements into the all-day Sunday service. This might include special worship sessions designed for families, where children and parents can worship together, sing songs, and engage in interactive activities that cater to different age groups. This allows families to bond spiritually and create lasting memories within the context of the service.

Additionally, intentional moments of family-centered teaching can be incorporated into the program. This could involve family devotionals or teachings that address topics relevant to parents and children alike, encouraging open dialogue and spiritual growth within the family unit. By providing resources and guidance, churches can support parents in their role as spiritual leaders and help foster a strong faith foundation within the family.

Furthermore, the fellowship aspect of the all-day Sunday service can be enriched by creating spaces and activities that cater to families. For example, a designated area with toys, games, and activities can be provided, allowing parents and children to engage in meaningful interaction and build connections with other families. This creates an environment where parents can relax and enjoy fellowship while their children play and socialize in a safe and supervised space.

To ensure families have the opportunity to experience the entire all-day Sunday service together, intentional scheduling and programming can be implemented. This might involve rotating activities and sessions to ensure that families have the opportunity to participate in worship, teaching, and fellowship as a unit. Clear communication and well-structured time slots can enable families to plan their day accordingly and make the most of the all-day service experience.

It is essential for churches to understand the unique needs and dynamics of families within their congregation and tailor their approach accordingly. Flexibility, support, and creativity are key in designing a family-friendly all-day Sunday service. By creating an inclusive and engaging environment that addresses the needs of both parents and children, churches can foster a sense of unity and provide families with the opportunity to grow in their faith together.

Chapter 8: Embracing Change and Growth

The implementation of an all-day Sunday service has the potential to bring about transformative change within churches and local communities. By embracing this new format, churches can position themselves to meet the evolving needs of their congregation, foster deeper spiritual engagement, and cultivate a vibrant and inclusive community.

Unlocking the potential for remarkable growth and development, the groundbreaking approach of an all-day Sunday service heralds a new era for churches and Christian communities. Within its innovative framework lie abundant opportunities for transformative change, offering a vibrant tapestry of possibilities.

The first stirring prospect lies in the realm of increased community engagement. The all-day Sunday service serves as a springboard, propelling individuals to actively participate and contribute their unique gifts to the flourishing tapestry of church life. Through its inclusive design, diverse voices resonate and are celebrated, nurturing a profound sense of belonging that permeates every facet of the community. This inclusivity unlocks a gateway to greater engagement, beckoning congregants to extend their involvement beyond the confines of the Sunday service, immersing themselves in various church activities and endeavors.

A powerful catalyst for deepening spiritual experiences, the all-day Sunday service grants worshippers the extraordinary freedom to forge their own path. Emboldened by the liberty to choose activities that resonate with their souls, individuals can sculpt their spiritual encounters with precision, harmonizing their yearnings with divine presence. This heightened engagement unfurls opportunities for personal growth, unveiling profound understandings of God's Word and fostering connections that breathe life into the communal fabric.

At the heart of this transformative model lies the expansion of ministry opportunities. Embarking on this journey, individuals are inspired to share their stories, teachings, and talents with an effervescent fervor. From this fertile ground springs forth an effusion of creativity, birthing specialized ministries tailored to meet the diverse needs and aspirations of the faithful. Within these newfound spheres, mentoring programs, outreach initiatives, and discipleship groups flourish, intertwining the lives of congregants and amplifying the transformative power of service.

The all-day Sunday service imbues a nurturing environment, fostering the growth of discipleship relationships. Here, seasoned church leaders and experienced believers find a fertile landscape to invest in the lives of others, guiding, supporting, and nurturing spiritual maturation. Within this extended timeframe, discipleship thrives, forging unbreakable bonds of accountability and illumination, propelling believers to new heights of faith.

Boundaries dissolve within the all-day Sunday service, birthing intergenerational connections that transcend time and wisdom. As participants of all ages gather in pursuit of spiritual growth, a rich tapestry of mentorship opportunities emerges. The dance of shared wisdom unfolds, as the younger generation drinks deeply from the wells of experience while the seasoned saints are invigorated by the unyielding zeal and vivacity of youth. Intergenerational connections transform the church into a haven where wisdom and vibrancy converge, breathing life into the collective journey of faith.

Mirroring the pulse of modern lifestyles, the all-day Sunday service extends an empathetic hand, accommodating the unique demands of today's fast-paced world. Embracing flexible timings and a diverse range of activities, it offers solace to those wrestling with work commitments, family obligations, and the complexities of modern existence. Within this sanctuary of inclusivity, the perennial barriers that previously hindered active participation crumble, ushering in a wave of congregants who reclaim their rightful place in the tapestry of church life.

A resplendent opportunity for evangelism and outreach unveils itself within the all-day Sunday service. With its compelling allure, it beckons the seeker and newcomer into an inviting and accessible space, brimming with the transformative power of a genuine Christian community. In this realm of diversity and interactivity, the curious are welcomed, their questions nurtured, and their souls enveloped in the arms of a loving fellowship. A powerful instrument for spreading the redemptive message of God's love, the all-day Sunday service bears the potential to ignite a wildfire of transformative encounters, as faithful congregants invite friends.

As churches embrace the all-day Sunday service and adapt it to their unique contexts, the possibilities for growth and development are vast. The key lies in remaining open to change, cultivating a spirit of innovation, and continuously seeking ways to deepen the impact of the church in the lives of individuals and the wider community. Through this transformative approach, churches can foster a vibrant, engaged, and relevant Christian community that reflects the love of Christ to the world.

Chapter 9: How To Start?

The concept of transitioning to an all-day Sunday service may seem like a monumental endeavor for many churches. However, starting with a one-time event to test the waters can be an excellent way to explore the feasibility and impact of this innovative approach within your own congregation. This trial run allows the church leadership and members to assess the benefits, challenges, and practical considerations involved in implementing an all-day Sunday service.

The first step in organizing a one-time event is to garner support and build a team of dedicated individuals who are passionate about exploring new possibilities for worship and community engagement. This team can consist of church leaders, volunteers, and members who are eager to contribute their time, talents, and ideas to make the event a success.

Planning and preparation are essential to ensure a smooth and impactful experience. Start by clearly defining the goals and objectives of the event. What are you hoping to achieve through the all-day Sunday service? Is it increased community engagement, deeper spiritual experiences, or the fostering of meaningful relationships? Aligning your vision and purpose will guide the planning process.

Consider the logistics of the event, such as the timing, venue, and resources needed. Determine whether the event will take place within the existing church premises or if an alternative space is required. Evaluate the availability of necessary facilities, such as separate rooms for worship, teaching, and fellowship, as well as child care arrangements if applicable. If additional resources or equipment are needed, explore options for borrowing, renting, or purchasing them.

Promote the event within your congregation by sharing the vision, goals, and anticipated benefits of the all-day Sunday service. Encourage active participation and invite individuals to contribute their ideas and talents. Create a buzz and excitement around the event to generate enthusiasm and support.

Craft a schedule that reflects the key components of the all-day Sunday service: worship, teaching, prayer, and fellowship. Determine the duration of each session, allowing for flexibility and breaks between activities. Consider incorporating a mix of live speakers, pre-recorded videos, and interactive elements to cater to different preferences and ensure a diverse experience.

Designate team members responsible for each aspect of the event, from worship and teaching coordination to logistics and hospitality. Encourage creativity and innovation in the planning process, considering ways to make the event engaging and impactful for attendees. Explore options for incorporating technology, visual aids, interactive elements, and multimedia presentations to enhance the worship and teaching experiences.

During the event, ensure that adequate support and assistance are available to address the needs of attendees. Volunteers can serve as guides, ushers, and hosts, providing a warm and welcoming atmosphere. Create a sense of unity and inclusion by encouraging attendees to actively participate in activities, engage in conversations, and connect with fellow members.

After the one-time event, it is crucial to evaluate its impact and gather feedback from the congregation. Conduct surveys, hold focus groups, or encourage individuals to share their experiences and suggestions for improvement. Assess the effectiveness of each component of the all-day Sunday service, including worship, teaching, prayer, and fellowship, and identify areas of strength and areas that may require further refinement.

Reflect on the overall success of the event, considering factors such as attendance, engagement levels, and the sense of community fostered. Use this feedback and evaluation to inform future planning and potential implementation of the all-day Sunday service as a regular offering within your church.

Remember, starting with a one-time event allows your church to experiment and adapt to this new format while minimizing potential risks and challenges. It provides an opportunity to gauge interest, gather insights, and make any necessary adjustments before committing to a more permanent transition.

By embarking on this trial run, your church can explore the transformative possibilities of an all-day Sunday service, nurturing deeper connections, enriching spiritual experiences, and fostering a vibrant and inclusive community. Embrace this opportunity to step into uncharted territory, where faith flourishes, and the transformative power of God's love is unleashed.

If you have a burning desire to host an extraordinary all-day church event, we are here to come alongside you and offer our unwavering support. We believe in the power of faith-filled events that uplift and inspire, and we want to help you make your vision a reality.

You see, we understand that organizing a remarkable all-day church event requires careful planning and attention to detail. But let me assure you, with the right guidance and resources, you can create a life-changing experience that will leave a lasting impact on your congregation and community.

So, here's what you need to do. Reach out to us, and let's connect. Share your vision, your dreams, and your aspirations for this all-day church event. We'll listen with open hearts and eager anticipation, ready to provide you with the guidance and support you need to make it all happen.

Our experienced team will work hand in hand with you to develop a comprehensive plan that aligns with your unique circumstances and goals. We'll help you design a captivating schedule, select the perfect venues, and coordinate all the logistics to ensure a seamless and unforgettable event.

But it doesn't stop there. We'll bring our wealth of knowledge and expertise to the table, offering you insightful suggestions on worship experiences that will uplift souls, teaching sessions that will ignite hearts, and interactive fellowship activities that will forge deeper connections within your community.

And let me tell you this when you mix prayer and promotion nothing can stop you! We'll equip you with effective marketing strategies, showing you how to use the power of social media and other platforms to spread the word and create a buzz around your all-day church event. We want people to feel the excitement, to sense the divine calling to attend and be transformed.

Now, let's talk resources. We understand that each church has its unique blessings and challenges. Whether you have a grand budget or more modest means, we'll tailor our support to meet your needs. We believe in making miracles happen, regardless of the size of your resources.

But our commitment doesn't end with the event itself, oh no. We are in this journey together. We'll stand by your side, providing ongoing support and guidance as you navigate through the implementation and execution of your vision. Our desire is to empower you to create a lasting impact in the lives of those who attend your all-day church event.

So, it's time to take that leap of faith. Reach out to us, and let's join forces to create an all-day church event that will leave a mark on hearts and transform lives. Together, we will witness the incredible power of God's love manifesting in the midst of your congregation and community.

In closing, I want you to know that we believe in you. We believe in the dreams and visions God has placed in your heart. Let's make them a reality. Contact us today, and let the journey of extraordinary faith-filled transformation begin.

Contact us at:
alldaychurchservice@gmail.com

Made in the USA
Las Vegas, NV
08 June 2023

73124954R00030